Elijah
Brave Prophet

ANGELINE J. ENTZ • ILLUSTRATED BY **H. DON FIELDS**

BROADMAN PRESS
Nashville, Tennessee

Dewey Decimal Classification: J221.92
Subject heading: ELIJAH

Printed in the United States of America

Contents

A Daring Mission

Elijah looked at the four square pillars of the palace gate. They were strong and dust-colored at the top of the hill. Once again he wondered how he could get inside. Still, God had sent him, and he was sure God would help him deliver his message.

Elijah stopped to rest for a moment. He could understand why Omri, Ahab's father, had chosen this hill for his capital. Its location made it hard for enemies to attack. And the view from this hilltop would surely make a king feel proud.

4

A blare of silver trumpets sounded, and Elijah saw a line of men and women dressed in bright clothing. They left the palace gate and filed toward a grove of trees on a nearby hilltop.

Disgust welled up in Elijah.

They were the priests and priestesses of Baal. They were going to offer sacrifices in the grove.

5

Ahab was king of Israel . . . he knew the laws of God, especially the one that said, "You must not worship any carved idols." But he and Queen Jezebel didn't obey Yahweh, the God of Abraham and Moses. They worshiped an idol named Baal. Baal was called the ruler of storms and rain.

Elijah reached the top of the hill as the last of the procession passed through the huge gates. Suddenly a wave of excitement swept through the crowd, and the guards began to shout and bow low.

Among the worshipers was Queen Jezebel in a beautiful robe of purple and scarlet. She was wearing a necklace with a gold pendant. It was a tiny figure of a man standing upon a bull, holding a sheaf of thunderbolts above his head.

Every eye was on the proud figure of the queen. In the excitement of the moment the guards didn't even notice Elijah. He slipped into the open courtyard and hurried through an ivory-tiled hallway toward the throne room.

Elijah's bare feet made no sound on the polished floor, and he was far into the room before the king saw him. Ahab started. He looked at the figure in the rough coat, with shaggy hair hanging about his shoulders and eyes flashing like fire.

"Ahab!" Elijah cried. "Here is a message from the Lord, the God of Israel. No rain will fall on your land for three years. The Lord will not send even a drop of dew."

Ahab turned red with anger and leaped to his feet. "Guards!" he shouted. "Guards, seize him!"

7

8

Elijah heard the sound of running feet, and he quickly escaped through an empty corridor. "Thank you, Lord," he whispered. He had managed to get into Ahab's palace and safely out again.

Several hours later Elijah looked out cautiously from the rocks where he had hidden. He watched as the sun sank behind the hills and darkness fell. Drawing his cloak around him, Elijah left his hiding place. If he expected to reach Tisbe by daybreak, he would have to keep up a swift pace.

It was past midnight before he reached the Jordan River. He felt safer when he reached Gilead. This was his boyhood home, and the hills and canyons offered many hiding places. He felt the wind blow, and he sniffed the good smell of acacia trees.

Shortly before sunrise he stopped beside a little brook called Cherith. He was hungry and tired, and a little afraid. He could not stay in any of the little villages. Ahab's soldiers might find him there. How could he get food in this lonely place?

Suddenly Elijah was startled by a flutter of black wings, and a raven flew to the ground at his feet. In its bill was a piece of bread.

"Thank you, Lord," Elijah prayed. "Forgive me for not trusting you more. I know you will take care of me."

Thinkback: What had Ahab and Jezebel done to displease God? What message did God send Elijah to deliver? How did God take care of Elijah?

Lightning Without Rain

The rumble of faraway thunder woke Elijah from an uneasy sleep. He walked around some rocks as he watched the lightning. The wind began to blow in gusts from the east. And Elijah felt the gritty sand whipped up from the desert.

Elijah turned and went back to his camp.

The month of Elul passed with more lightning, but no rain fell. The time of barley planting came, but the earth was dry and hard. "It's a waste of seed to plant before the winter rains," the farmers told one another.

The leaves withered on the broom plants, and the juniper trees faded from green to grey. The pastures dried up, and the few crops still standing in the fields died and blew away in the dry whirlwinds. The sheep and goats searched for clumps of dry grass to eat.

Elijah watched the brook Cherith day after day. The hot·sun was drying up the water. The few goats that came to drink were thin and shabby. The wild animals and birds could find little to eat.

The month of Chislev came with cooler weather, but the west wind brought no rain. The farmers looked anxiously toward Lebanon, but they could see no new snow on the mountaintops.

Early the next morning Elijah drew his cloak around him and set out. Surely he was wrong about what the Lord told him to do. He knew he had to leave Gilead. But should he really go north, to Zarephath in the land of Sidon? Should he enter the homeland of Queen Jezebel? Surely that was not the sensible thing to do. And yet, the Lord's guidance was so clear.

Without looking back, Elijah set his face to the north, toward the village of Zarephath.

Thinkback: Why did Elijah have to leave Gilead? Where did the Lord tell him to go? Why was Elijah surprised at this instruction?

Hiding Place in Zarephath

"Will you give me a drink of water?"
Elijah asked the woman gathering
firewood outside the gates of Zarephath.

The woman turned in surprise. She was
very thin and stooped. Elijah saw she was
much younger than he first thought.

16

As the woman moved toward the gate, Elijah said, "And also bring me some bread to eat."

A long moment passed as the woman stared at him. "I know you are a servant of the true God," she said finally, "and I would like to help you. But I have no bread in my house. In fact, I have only a little olive oil left and a small amount of flour. Just enough to make one more loaf of bread. I'm gathering wood to bake this bread for my son and me. When it's gone, we'll die."

"Don't worry," Elijah said. "Make the loaf of bread for me, and then make one for yourself and your son. God will provide for you."

Without a word the woman turned and walked into the town. Elijah followed her to a narrow house on a twisting street. The heavy wooden door opened directly onto the street. A steep stairway led up to a small room on the roof.

The woman went to a small courtyard at the back of the house. She lit a fire with the sticks she had gathered and set a flat stone to heating. From a clay jar she took a handful of coarse flour. She scraped the inside and finally tipped the jar to pour every grain onto a kneading board. Quickly she added a measure of olive oil and kneaded the flour into a flat cake. Then she placed it on the heated stone.

18

While it cooked, she went to a large waterpot and poured a cup of cool water. When the bread had cooked, she silently handed the water and loaf to Elijah.

He bowed his head and gave thanks. When he looked up, the woman was still standing in the same place, watching him.

"Why don't you take some flour and make a loaf for your son and yourself?" Elijah asked.

The woman stared at him and started to speak. Then she went to the flour jar and poured out the flour. There was just enough flour for one more loaf.

Elijah smiled to himself. Perhaps the woman didn't believe it, but Elijah knew that there would be flour and oil each day for as long as it was needed.

Thinkback: How did God take care of Elijah in Zarephath? How was the widow rewarded for her kindness to Elijah?

Challenge to Ahab

Three years had passed, and Elijah and Ahab stood face to face again.

"So you're back again, you troublemaker!" Ahab scowled. "Haven't you caused enough problems for Israel?"

"You are the one who has brought the trouble, not me." Elijah looked at King Ahab. "You and your family have forgotten God's laws, and you have worshiped false gods and idols."

Elijah looked around at the king's guards and followers. He raised his voice so all of them could hear. "Listen to me," he commanded. "Call all the Israelites to the top of Mount Carmel. Also, call for the prophets of Baal and Asherah."

When the people had come together, Elijah looked around. He saw people who had once worshiped Yahweh, the God who brought their ancestors out of the land of Egypt. Now these people had turned from God, and worshiped Jezebel's god, the idol Baal.

"Why won't you make up your minds?" Elijah shouted. "If Yahweh the Lord is God, worship him. But if Baal is god, then follow him."

The people stared at Elijah. His shaggy beard and rough cloak were covered with dust. Then they looked at the four hundred priests of Baal. They were dressed in the rich robes and golden jewelry given to them by Queen Jezebel. No one dared say a word.

"Bring two bulls to be offered as sacrifices," Elijah ordered. "Let the priests of Baal kill one and place it upon their altar. But do not light a fire to burn the sacrifice. I will kill the other bull and place it upon the altar of the Lord, God of Israel. And whichever sends fire to his sacrifice, let Israel worship him."

The crowd agreed. First the prophets of Baal killed their bull, cut it up, and placed in on a huge pile of firewood. Then they began to pray to Baal.

"Baal, Baal, answer us," they shouted. "Answer, O lord of sky and weather, answer." Around and round the altar they danced, shouting and waving their arms. Clouds of dust billowed around their feet.

Three hours passed, and the sun stood directly overhead. The sky was hot and dull.

"Baal, answer us! Baal, answer us!"

"Why don't you shout a little louder?"
Elijah called to Baal's priests. "He may be
thinking or busy with something else. Or
perhaps he's away on a journey."

Baal's priests screamed louder. Their
voices were hoarse with hours of
shouting. Their dancing grew even wilder.

"Perhaps he's asleep," Elijah laughed.
"Try to wake him up."

Some of the priests took knives and
swords and cut themselves. They hoped
Baal would answer when he saw their blood.

All afternoon they screamed and
danced. Sweat, dust, and blood stained
their fine robes. But Baal did not answer.

At last Elijah called to the people, "Come here." They watched in silence as he built up the altar of Yahweh, which King Ahab had destroyed. Elijah used twelve large stones to represent the twelve tribes of Israel which the Lord had brought out of Egypt years before.

He placed wood on the altar. Then he stacked on the wood the pieces of the bull he killed. Around the altar he dug a deep ditch.

Last of all, he ordered men to fill four large water jars and to pour the water over the sacrifice.

"Fill the water jars again," he called. The water soaked into the dry wood.

Three times the men poured water over the sacrifice. Finally the water ran down and filled the trench around the altar.

Then Elijah knelt before the altar. Quietly he prayed: "Lord God of Abraham, Isaac, and Jacob, let these people know that you are God. Let them know that I am following your commands. Lord God, answer my prayer."

With a loud crack, as though the heavens had split, fire fell from God. It burned the sacrifice, the wood, and the altar. It even dried up the water in the trench.

The people bowed down in fear and awe. "The Lord is God," they shouted. "Yahweh is God."

"You can eat and drink now," Elijah told King Ahab. "I hear the sound of rain."

Ahab looked at the clear sky. He could see no sign of rain. Slowly he returned to his chariot.

Elijah stood on the top of Mount Carmel. He looked out across the blue Mediterranean Sea. Then he knelt and prayed.

After a while he told his servant, "Go look to the west, and tell me what you see."

"I see nothing but the sky and the sea," the servant answered.

Again Elijah prayed. Then he told his servant, "Go look to the west."

"I see only the sea and the sky," the servant said.

Some of the people who had seen the fire fall began to whisper, "Baal is the lord of rain and storm. Perhaps only he can send rain."

Elijah prayed again.

A few of the people who had bowed down to Yahweh a little while before began to wonder, "The Lord Yahweh can make fire fall from heaven, but perhaps he can't make it rain."

Elijah tried to shut out the sound of their voices as he prayed. "Lord God, I have obeyed your commands. You told me that you would send rain, and I believe you. I trust you to keep your word."

Seven times Elijah sent his servant to look to the west. Six times the answer was the same.

The seventh time the servant replied, "I see a cloud no bigger than a man's hand."

"Run to the king," Elijah ordered. "Tell him to hurry to his palace before the rain comes."

31

Billowy clouds began to gather, and the sky grew dark. Elijah drew his robes about him and fastened them tightly.

Strong winds blew and a few drops of rain fell. Elijah began to run down the road to Jezreel.

Faster and faster and harder and harder the rain pounded the parched earth. Faster and faster through the rain and wind Elijah ran. He passed the rain-drenched king huddled in his speeding chariot.

"Praise to Yahweh, the Almighty," Elijah shouted. "Praise to the Lord."

Thinkback: Why did it take courage for Elijah to challenge the priests of Baal?

How did he show courage when he prayed for rain?

Imagine you are Elijah. How did you feel when you challenged Ahab? When you prayed for rain seven times? When you were running to Jezreel?

A Frightened Prophet

Elijah and his servant crept out of the city in darkness. They did not even take time to bring food for the journey.

Jezebel had been furious when she learned what happened on Mount Carmel. She vowed, "Before another day passes, that preacher of God, Elijah will be dead!"

Jezebel is rich and powerful, with hundreds of servants to obey her, Elijah thought. *I am poor and have no powerful friends to help me. What shall I do?*

All that night Elijah and his servant walked toward the south. By the next sunset they reached Bethel. There Jacob had once slept with a stone for his pillow and had dreamed of a ladder to heaven. But Elijah was afraid to stop.

During the next night, Elijah and his servant passed Jerusalem. *I can't stop here,* Elijah thought. *Jehoshaphat, the king of Judah, serves the Lord, but he has made a pledge of friendship with Ahab.*

About dawn they reached Beer-sheba, at the southern end of Judah. They had walked more than eighty-five miles without food or sleep. Elijah left his servant and went into the desert alone.

35

It was very hot, and Elijah was tired and
weak. At last he had to stop. He lay down
under a small juniper bush and prayed:
"Lord, I'm no use to you any more. I can't
keep on fighting Jezebel, as weak as I am.
She has thousands of followers, and I am
only one man. I'm too tired to go on. Let
me die, right now." While Elijah was
praying, he fell into a deep sleep.

When he woke, the sun was rising. Near him burned a little fire, with a round loaf cooking on the hot stones. A pitcher of cool water stood near. Elijah looked around in surprise.

He saw a tall man who told him, "Rise and eat."

Elijah thought, *This must be a messenger from God.* When Elijah had eaten, he lay down again and slept. Again he woke to find food, and the angel again invited him to eat.

Elijah needed food and rest after his long journey from Mount Carmel. He also needed new courage. "Go to Mount Sinai," the angel told him.

For forty days Elijah traveled in the desert. He looked up at the mountain and remembered that it was called "the mountain of the Lord." It was there that Moses received the Ten Commandments.

As Elijah wandered in the desert, God spoke to him, "Why are you here, Elijah?"

"Because I serve you, Lord," Elijah answered. "The people of Israel have forgotten their promises to obey you. They have killed your prophets, and I'm the only one left who still follows you."

"Go up onto the mountain," God commanded. As Elijah climbed, a strong wind swirled around him. Dust burned his eyes. Finally, he groped his way into a cave among the rocks.

As the wind blew stronger, trees swayed and fell. Elijah heard the sharp crack as they broke. *Surely,* Elijah thought, *God intends to give me a message through this mighty storm.*

Then as the storm began to calm, Elijah felt the ground shaking. The whole mountain trembled with a great earthquake. Large rocks tore loose and rolled past the cave where Elijah hid. Still God did not speak.

After the earthquake a fire broke out, but the Lord's message was not in the fire. At last, Elijah heard a voice of gentle stillness. Covering his face in awe, he crept to the entrance of the cave.

"Why are you here, Elijah?" asked the quiet voice of the Lord. "I have much more for you to do. Go back to your own land. I still have many people in Israel who worship and obey me. You are not alone. Go on with your work for me."

Thinkback: Why was Elijah afraid?
How did God care for Elijah in the desert?
How did God give new courage to Elijah?

Elijah Chooses a Helper

Elijah walked along the road near the village of Abel-meholah. Twelve yokes of oxen were pulling plows, preparing the rich soil for planting. Elijah saw that one of the men driving the oxen was Elisha. He was the son of a prosperous farmer.

Elisha was the young man who would someday take Elijah's place as prophet. There were many things Elijah would have to teach Elisha before the young man would be ready to begin his work.

Elijah unfastened the shaggy cloak from his shoulders and placed it upon the shoulders of Elisha. The young farmer turned in surprise and looked at the old prophet. Elisha realized that God was calling him to become a prophet, also.

"Do I have time to go tell my father and mother good-bye?" he asked.

"Do as you wish," Elijah replied. "You must decide for yourself what you will do with your life."

Elisha unhitched his oxen and led them back to his parents' home. He broke the wooden yoke into firewood and offered the oxen as a sacrifice to God. "Never again will I return to my old life as a farmer," he said. "From this time, I will be a servant of God."

Then Elisha hurried down the road to catch up with Elijah. "Let me travel with you, sir. I want to learn how to obey God better. I will be your servant and help you."

The old prophet and the young one traveled together, preaching throughout Israel. "Destroy your idols!" they proclaimed. "Serve only God, and obey his commands."

At last the time came when Elijah knew his work was finished. He set out on the long road south from Gilgal.

Elijah tried to discourage his young friend from coming with him. "The Lord has sent me to Jericho. Why don't you wait here." But Elisha wanted to go with his old teacher.

43

As the two men came to the Jordan River, Elijah removed his cloak, folded it, and struck the river. The waters separated, and a path of dry ground appeared across the riverbed.

When they reached the other side, Elijah turned to his friend. "What can I give you as a gift, before I am taken away?"

"If it pleases God," Elisha said, "I would like to serve God as his prophet, just as you have done."

"You have chosen a hard task," the old prophet said. "If the Lord allows you to see me as I am being taken, it will mean that he has granted your request."

As they walked on, a chariot of fire, drawn by horses of fire, came between them, and Elijah was taken by a whirlwind into heaven.

When Elisha realized his old friend was gone, tears filled his eyes. *He was like a father to me,* he thought. *He was of more value to Israel than all its chariots and soldiers. What will we do without him?*

Then Elisha saw Elijah's cloak, the symbol of his authority, lying on the ground where it had fallen. As he picked up the cloak, Elisha thought about what had happened after he left his father's farm to follow God.

Elisha knew he must take his teacher's place as God's spokesman to Israel. At the riverbank he struck the river with the cloak, as Elijah had done. He said, "Where is the Lord, the God of Elijah?" At his words, the water divided, and Elisha crossed on dry ground.

Elisha began to climb the steep path that led up from the Jordan River. He was ready to carry on the work of the Lord.

Thinkback: How did Elisha know God wanted him to be a prophet and work with Elijah? What did Elisha do before he became a prophet? What are some things Elijah taught Elisha?

Reflections

Elijah was a brave prophet. Does this mean that he was never afraid? Can you remember some problems he had? How did he have the courage to face danger?

Think of times when you feel afraid. How can you have courage in times of danger?

When you think about the brave deeds of Elijah, does he seem like a superhuman person? James was a New Testament writer who lived eight hundred years after Elijah. James wrote, "Elijah was the same kind of person as we are. He prayed earnestly that there would be no rain, and no rain fell on the land for three and a half years. Once again he prayed, and the sky poured out its rain and the earth produced its crops" (James 5:17–18, TEV).*

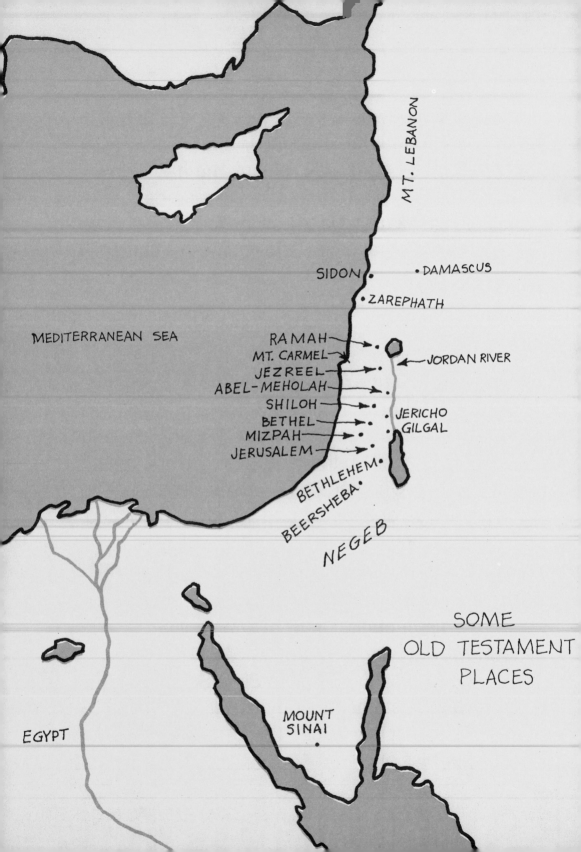

MT. LEBANON

SIDON •   • DAMASCUS

• ZAREPHATH

MEDITERRANEAN SEA

RAMAH →•
MT. CARMEL →•   ← JORDAN RIVER
JEZREEL →•
ABEL-MEHOLAH →•
SHILOH →•
BETHEL →•   JERICHO
MIZPAH →•   • GILGAL
JERUSALEM →•
              BETHLEHEM •
          BEERSHEBA •

                    NEGEB

SOME
OLD TESTAMENT
PLACES

EGYPT

MOUNT
SINAI
•